W9-CPE-166

THE BIG BOOK OF
THE BRAIN

ALL ABOUT THE BODY'S CONTROL CENTER

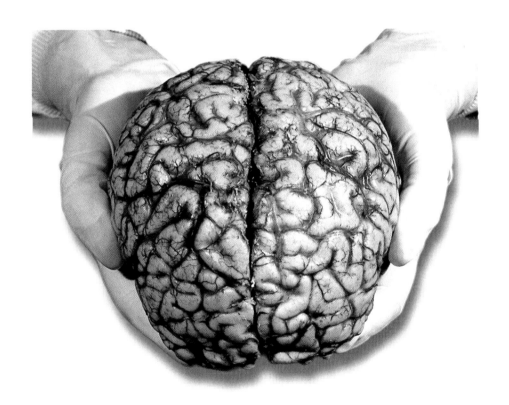

John Farndon

PETER BEDRICK BOOKS
NTC/Contemporary Publishing Group
NEW YORK

This U.S. edition first published in 2000 by

Peter Bedrick Books

a division of NTC/Contemporary Publishing Group

4255 West Touhy Avenue

Lincolnwood (Chicago), Illinois 60712-1975 USA

First published in Great Britain in 2000

by Hodder Wayland,

an imprint of Hodder Children's Books.

Hodder Children's Books

A division of Hodder Headline plc

338 Euston Road, London NW1 3BH

© Hodder Wayland 2000

Text © John Farndon 2000

Produced by:

Roger Coote Publishing,

Gissings Farm, Fressingfield,

Suffolk, IP21 5SH,

UK

Cover design: Roger Coote

Inside design: Sarah Crouch

Editor: Steve Setford

Consultant: Dr Alasdair Coles, Assistant Registrar,

Department of Neurology, Norfolk & Norwich Hospital

Printed and bound in Portugal

ISBN 0-658-01071-9

Library of Congress Cataloging-in-Publication Data

Farndon, John.

    The big book of the brain : all about the body's control center / John Farndon.- [1st

U.S. ed.].

       p. cm.

    Originally published: Great Britain : Hodder Way, 2000.

    ISBN 0-658-01071-9

    1. Brain-Popular works. I. Title.

QP376.F355 2000

613.8'2dc21

                     00-37904

Picture acknowledgments

Action-Plus Photographic 25 bottom (Mike Hewitt); Digital Stock 7 top
right, 8 bottom, 10 bottom, 13 top, 13 bottom, 15 bottom left, 15 bottom
right, 26 top, 28 centre, 38 bottom, 39 bottom; Digital Vision 13 centre, 19
bottom; Hodder Wayland 35 bottom; Images Colour Library *front cover*
(Masterfile); Science Photo Library 5, 8 top (Geoff Tompkinson), 9 bottom
(CNRI), 16 top right (Pr S.Cinti/CNRI), 25 top left, 25 top centre (Sheila
Terry), 27 bottom left (Bill Longcore), 27 bottom right (William Ervin), 29
right (Montreal Neuro Institute/McGill University/CNRI), 30 bottom, 31
top right (Jonathan Watts), 33 middle (Professors P.M. Motta, K.R. Porter,
& P.M. Andrews), 36 bottom right (Montreal Neuro Institute/McGill
University/CNRI), 40 top (Phillippe Plailly), 40 centre (James Holmes), 42
top (Damien Lovegrove); The Stock Market 7 bottom left (Lester
Lefkowitz), 11 top (Chuck Savage), 18 bottom (Lester Lefkowitz), 21 top
(Tom Stewart), 38 bottom (Michael Keller); Tony Stone 10 top (Stewart
Choen), 17 top (Chris Harvey), 17 bottom (Joe Mcbride), 20 bottom (Mike
Timo), 22 bottom left (Laurence Monneret), 23 top right (Alan
Abramowitz), 35 centre left (Jon Riley), 35 top right (Mark Hamil), 37 top
(Hunter Freeman), 37 bottom, 39 top (Bob Thomas), 43 (David Young
Wolf). The following artworks are by Michael Courtney: 7 centre left, centre
right and bottom right, 14, 18 top, 24, 26 bottom, 30/31, 31 bottom right.
All other artworks are by Alex Pang.

CONTENTS

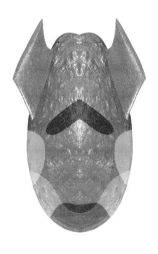

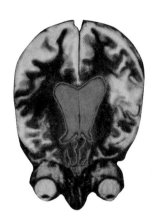

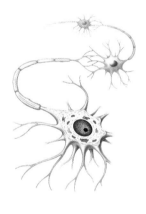

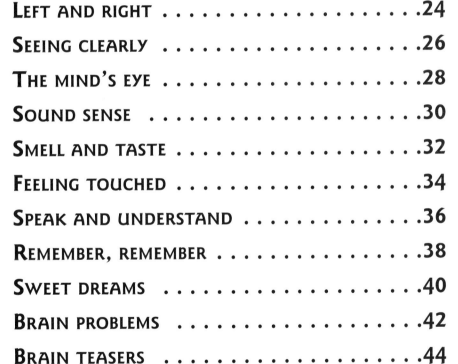

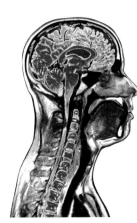

Words in **bold** are explained in the glossary.

WHAT IS A BRAIN?

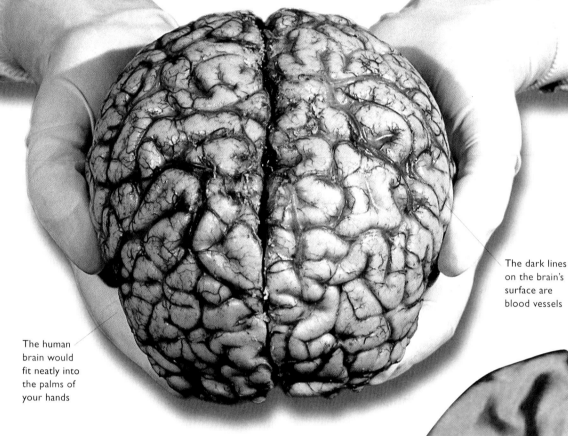

The human brain would fit neatly into the palms of your hands

Left In this picture, which illustrates the size of an average human brain, the brain's wrinkled surface is clearly visible.

Below This picture, made by a MRI (magnetic resonance imaging) scanner, gives an overhead view of a "slice" through the head. The eyes are at the bottom of the picture. MRI scans do not show bone – the yellow line around the edge is a layer of fat outside the skull.

The dark lines on the brain's surface are blood vessels

Inside your head is one of the most amazing objects in the universe: a human brain. If you could look under your skull and get a glimpse of your brain, you would see a grey lump like a walnut and about the same size as two potatoes. Yet this strange-looking thing allows you to think, love, eat, sleep, wake up, run, jump, play sport, watch TV… everything, in fact, that makes you human.

Animal brains

Humans are not the only creatures with brains. In fact, virtually every animal has a brain of some kind. A brain enables a creature to control its body and respond to situations as they arise – whether it is working out how to get round an obstacle, fleeing from danger, or finding food. The brain is linked to the body by threads called **nerves**, which send the brain information about what's going on in and around the body. The brain responds by sending out orders along other nerves to make the body do something.

How brains compare

Humans have brains that are much bigger in relation to their bodies than other animals, even though elephants and whales have much bigger brains overall. The human brain is special compared to the brains of other animals because of the size of the top portion of the brain, called the **cerebral cortex**, where the neurons are most densely packed. The human brain is nearly all cortex, a cat has a much smaller cortex and a fish has virtually no cortex at all.

Apes have a larger cortex for their size than any other creature except humans.

Fish brains are very small. The area dealing with smell reaches to the tip of the fish's nose

Compared to birds, cats have a much bigger cortex – the "clever" part of the brain. Perhaps that's why they catch them so often!

In proportion to the rest of the brain, the human cortex's surface area is larger than in other animals, because it is much more wrinkly

In a bird, the back of the brain, which controls balance and movement, is quite big. This part of the brain is essential to help them fly

Big brain

Your body is made up of billions of tiny living units called cells. Cells come in many different shapes and sizes, and many different kinds. Your brain and nerves are made up of spidery nerve cells, or **neurons**, all linked together like the circuits of an unbelievably complex computer. The human brain has about 15 billion neurons, compared to 100,000 or so for an insect and just 162 for a tapeworm.

Ape to human

Hominids, our earliest ancestors, lived more than four million years ago and were as much like apes as they were like humans. Only gradually did they evolve into humans like us. *Australopithecus*, the first hominids, had tiny brains – about 450 cubic centimetres (cc) in volume, much the same size as apes' brains today. But as hominids evolved, their brains got bigger. *Homo habilis* (Handy Man) lived 2 million years ago and had a brain of 750 cc. *Homo erectus* (Upright Man), who lived 1.5 million years ago had a brain of 1,000 cc. Neanderthal man, who lived 100,000 years ago – just

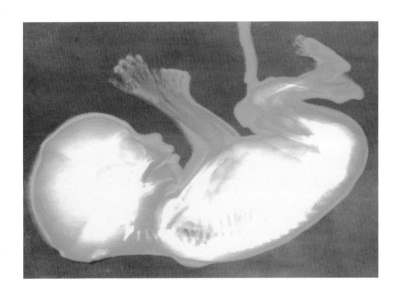

Above A human baby has to grow 15 billion neurons while it is developing in its mother's womb. In just one minute it can grow well over 100,000 neurons! After just four months in the womb, a baby already has enough of a brain to swallow, frown and suck its thumb.

before humans appeared – had a brain of about 1,500 cc. This is slightly larger than ours, which are about 1,400 cc on average, although our brains have a larger surface area because they are more wrinkled.

Brain Atlas

At first sight, the brain looks like it is all much the same – just a large, spongy, grey mass. But scientists have gradually worked out that its structure is actually quite varied, and that different things go on in different parts of the brain.

A brain of two halves

The most obvious thing about the brain is that it is split into two halves, or hemispheres. The left and right hemispheres are separated by a deep groove, but a huge bundle of nerves called the **corpus callosum** bridges the gap and keeps the two halves in touch. There are three main regions on each side of the brain. Deep in the middle of the brain, connected to the nerves in your spine, is the root of the brain, called the **brain stem**. This is where basic body functions such as breathing and heart rate are controlled, without you being aware of what's happening. Just behind the mid-brain, the top part of the brain stem, is a lump about the size of an apricot, called the **cerebellum**. This controls balance and co-ordination.

Top of the brain

The third and largest area of the brain is the **cerebrum**, which wraps around the mid-brain like a plum around its pit. This is where you think and where complicated tasks such as speaking, reading and conscious control of movements go on. The cerebrum is divided into four parts called cerebral **lobes**.

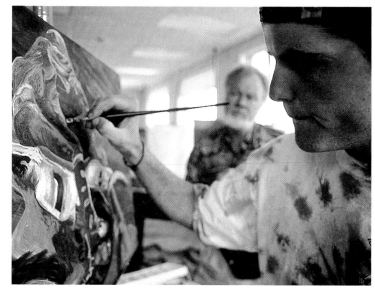

Above Moving a paint brush depends on messages from the senses – touch and sight – reaching the cerebral cortex, and the cortex sending messages back to muscles. But the creation of a picture depends on the 'clever' parts of the brain – the **lobes** (ends) of the cerebrum.

The cerebrum has a wrinkly outer surface, rather like the rind on a very shrivelled orange. This is called the cerebral cortex or grey matter. The cortex is where all the messages from the senses are received by the brain, and where all the brain's commands to the body are sent out.

Left The amazing balance of gymnasts – and the less amazing balance of everyone else – depends on the cerebellum, a special region at the back of the brain.

Above You feel like eating when the hypothalamus, a tiny area deep in the brain, sends out chemical hunger signals.

BRAIN POWER!

- The largest brain in the world belongs to the sperm whale. Its brain weighs 20 pounds, but this is just 0.02% of its body weight.
- The average human brain weighs 3 pounds – not much compared to a sperm whale's, but it makes up 2% of a person's body weight.
- About 85% of your brain's weight is water.
- Each minute roughly one quart of blood passes through the brain.
- Flattened out, the cerebral cortex would cover an office desk.

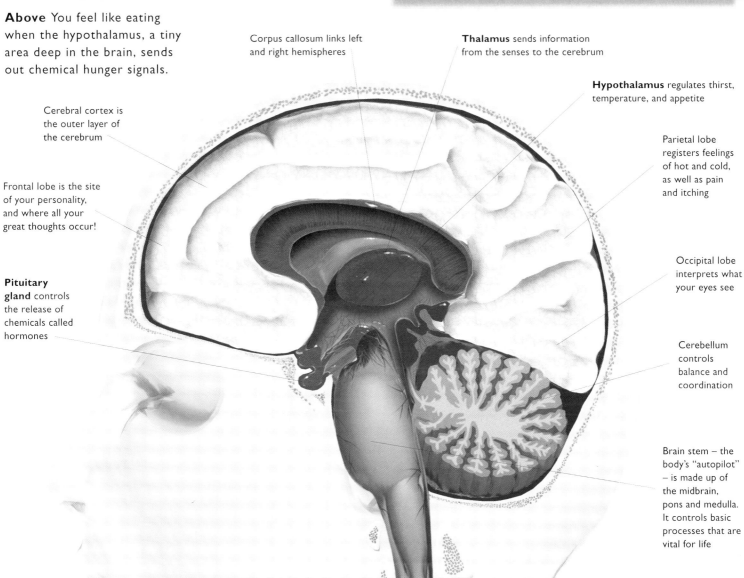

Corpus callosum links left and right hemispheres

Thalamus sends information from the senses to the cerebrum

Hypothalamus regulates thirst, temperature, and appetite

Cerebral cortex is the outer layer of the cerebrum

Parietal lobe registers feelings of hot and cold, as well as pain and itching

Frontal lobe is the site of your personality, and where all your great thoughts occur!

Occipital lobe interprets what your eyes see

Pituitary gland controls the release of chemicals called hormones

Cerebellum controls balance and coordination

Brain stem – the body's "autopilot" – is made up of the midbrain, pons and medulla. It controls basic processes that are vital for life

Left The brain is made up of nerve cells, but they are bundled together in different ways in different parts of the brain. Each nerve bundle has its own special task to perform.

GETTING NERVOUS

Your brain is linked to the rest of your body by the nervous system – an amazing network of nerves, all strung together like a miniature telephone network and constantly buzzing with activity. Every second, millions of nerve signals reach the brain from the body's sense organs (eyes, ears and so on). Every second, too, almost as many whizz out from the brain telling the body what to do.

The focus of all this nerve activity, and the main information highway for signals to travel to and from the brain, is the **spinal cord** – an amazing bundle of nerves running right down your backbone or spine. This, together with the brain, make up what is sometimes called the **central nervous system**, or CNS. Spreading out from the spinal cord to every other part of the body, like the branches of a tree, is the peripheral nervous system, or PNS.

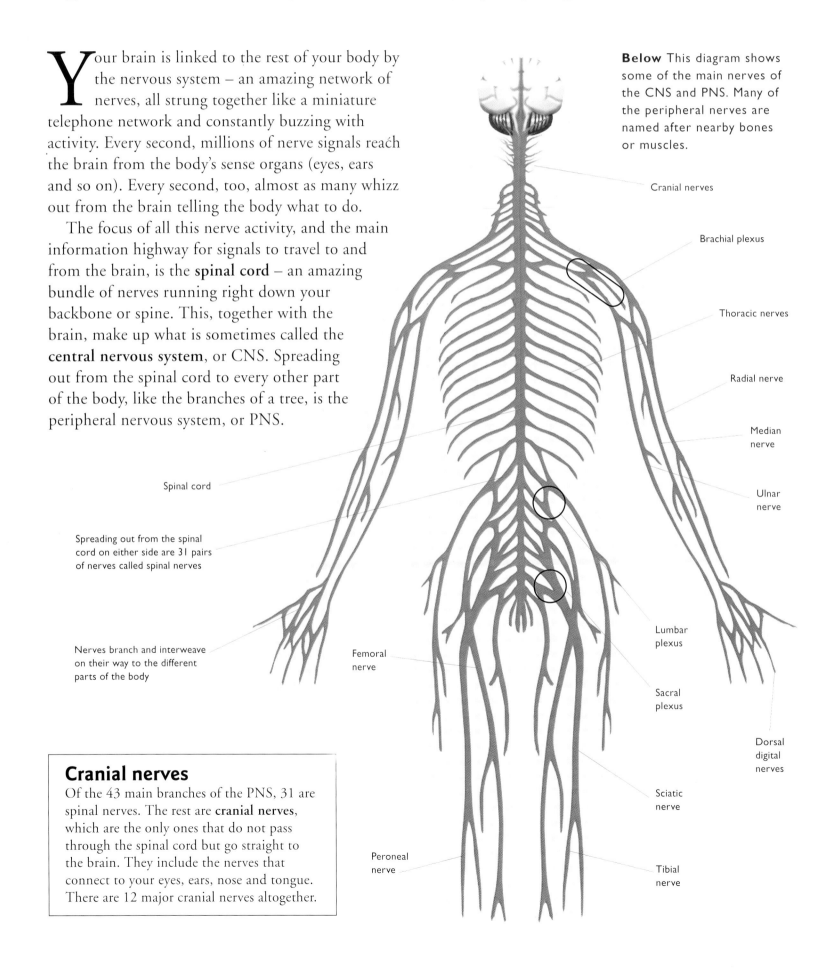

Below This diagram shows some of the main nerves of the CNS and PNS. Many of the peripheral nerves are named after nearby bones or muscles.

Cranial nerves

Brachial plexus

Thoracic nerves

Radial nerve

Median nerve

Ulnar nerve

Spinal cord

Spreading out from the spinal cord on either side are 31 pairs of nerves called spinal nerves

Nerves branch and interweave on their way to the different parts of the body

Femoral nerve

Lumbar plexus

Sacral plexus

Dorsal digital nerves

Sciatic nerve

Peroneal nerve

Tibial nerve

Cranial nerves

Of the 43 main branches of the PNS, 31 are spinal nerves. The rest are **cranial nerves**, which are the only ones that do not pass through the spinal cord but go straight to the brain. They include the nerves that connect to your eyes, ears, nose and tongue. There are 12 major cranial nerves altogether.

Left To hit a tennis ball, your nervous system must feed the brain a string of signals about the position of your arm and the moving ball, and your brain must send signals to move the right muscles.

Below When the starting gun fires, a cranial nerve relays the sound from the athlete's ear to his brain. His brain sends signals via the spinal nerves to launch him off the starting blocks.

BRAIN POWER!

- The longest nerve, the sciatic nerve, runs from the base of the spine to the ankle.
- Some peripheral nerves are as wide as your thumb.
- Groups of nerve-cell bodies are called ganglia. Bundles of interweaving nerves are called plexuses.
- The solar plexus, behind the stomach, is the biggest nerve network in the ANS.
- The sympathetic nervous system was once thought to respond to sufferings and feelings.

Inner nerves

Besides the CNS and PNS, your body has a third nervous system – a system you are not even aware of, but which is just as important. This is the **autonomic nervous system**, or ANS. It controls all the body processes and parts that go on or function automatically without you thinking about them, such as breathing, heartbeat, digestion, blood pressure and some glands. The ANS continually feeds information back to the brain, and the brain continually sends out orders for the heart to beat faster, the lungs to breathe slower, and so on.

Keeping the body stable

The ANS itself is split into two different parts: the sympathetic and the parasympathetic nervous systems. The parasympathetic system consists of nerves that branch off from each end of the CNS – that is, from your head and from the base of your spine. It gets its orders from the region of the brain called the brain stem. The parasympathetic system acts as a kind of brake on the body's parts and processes, sending signals telling them to slow down and work at a normal pace.

The sympathetic system is made of nerves that branch off the spinal cord between the neck and the small of the back. It gets its orders from the region of the brain called the hypothalamus. The sympathetic system speeds up the body and its processes, when it needs to be very active or is under stress. Because the two parts of the ANS produce opposite effects, they help to keep the body in a stable state.

NERVE CELLS

Your nervous system consists of long strings of special nerve cells, called neurons, all linked together, like beads on a necklace. Most of the body's cells are quite short-lived, and are always being replaced by new ones. But neurons live for a long time – which is a good thing, because after you are born, no new ones will ever grow!

The body's cells are like small parcels. Each contains a tiny control centre called a nucleus. Neurons, too, have a nucleus, but they also have a long winding "tail" called an **axon**, ending in tiny branching threads called dendrites.

Below A typical neuron has a cell body with tentacle-like dendrites and a long "tail," called an axon. Just as tiny wires carry electrical signals around the circuits of a computer, axons and dendrites carry electrical nerve signals all over the body.

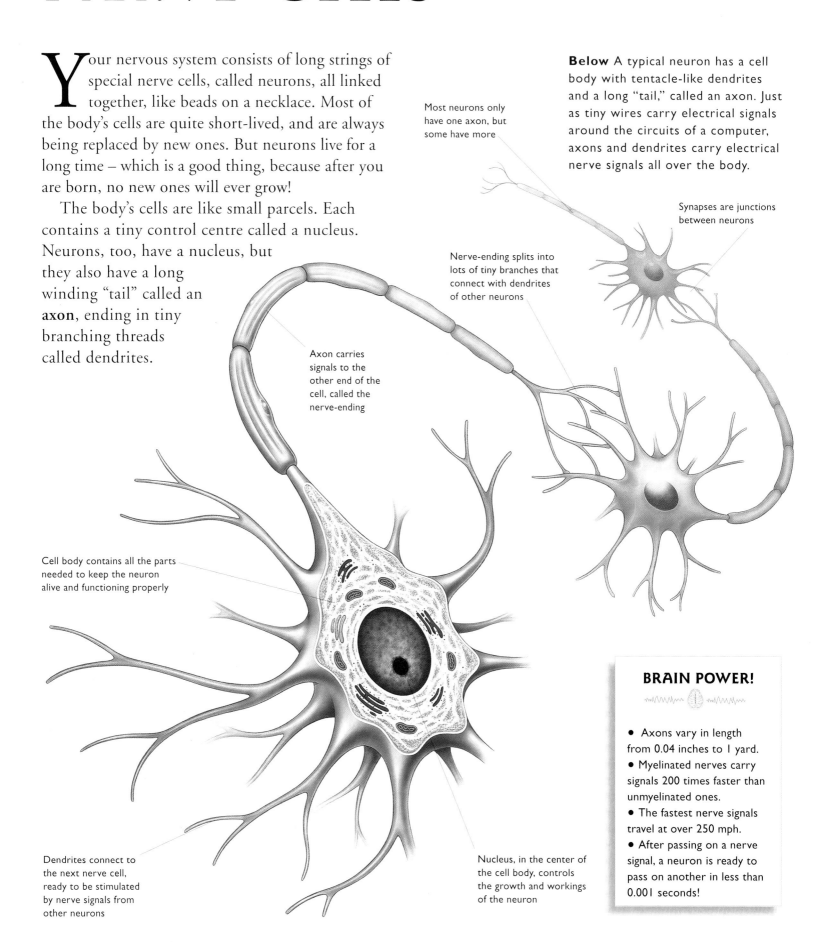

Most neurons only have one axon, but some have more

Synapses are junctions between neurons

Nerve-ending splits into lots of tiny branches that connect with dendrites of other neurons

Axon carries signals to the other end of the cell, called the nerve-ending

Cell body contains all the parts needed to keep the neuron alive and functioning properly

Dendrites connect to the next nerve cell, ready to be stimulated by nerve signals from other neurons

Nucleus, in the center of the cell body, controls the growth and workings of the neuron

BRAIN POWER!

- Axons vary in length from 0.04 inches to 1 yard.
- Myelinated nerves carry signals 200 times faster than unmyelinated ones.
- The fastest nerve signals travel at over 250 mph.
- After passing on a nerve signal, a neuron is ready to pass on another in less than 0.001 seconds!

What's in a nerve

Most nerve cells are bundled together to make the major nerves of your nervous system. About 1 in 100 nerves – the "sensory" nerves that take messages from the senses to your brain – are made up of neurons whose nucleus is at one end of the axon. About 1 in 10 nerves – the "motor" nerves that take messages from the brain to your muscles – are made up of neurons whose nucleus is in the middle of the axon. The other nerves in the CNS are made up of **interneurons** – nerve cells with very short axons.

Sending signals

Nerve signals enter a neuron through its dendrites and rush along the axon. At the far end, called the nerve-ending, the axon has other dendrites that pass the message on to the dendrites of other neurons.

Neurons that have to carry urgent signals over long distances are surrounded by thick insulation to keep the signal strong, in the same way that the cable from a TV aerial to the TV is coated with insulating plastic. In the case of neurons, the insulation is a myelin sheath – a series of long, flat cells wrapped around the axon. In people with the crippling disease multiple sclerosis, the sheaths break down, weakening the nerve signals.

How nerve signals move

Nerve signals can travel thanks to the electrical difference between the inside and outside of a neuron: outside is an excess of sodium ions (particles), which have a positive electric charge; inside is an excess of negatively charged potassium ions. The membrane (skin) of the neuron prevents sodium ions rushing in to balance out the charges. When a nerve signal arrives, tiny gateways open in the membrane. Sodium seeps into the cell, causing gateways to open further along the nerve. This, in turn, lets in more sodium ions, opening even more gateways, and so the signal passes along the nerve.

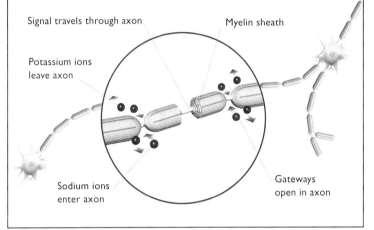

Signal travels through axon

Myelin sheath

Potassium ions leave axon

Sodium ions enter axon

Gateways open in axon

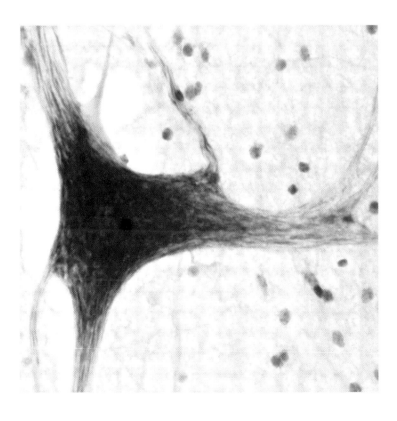

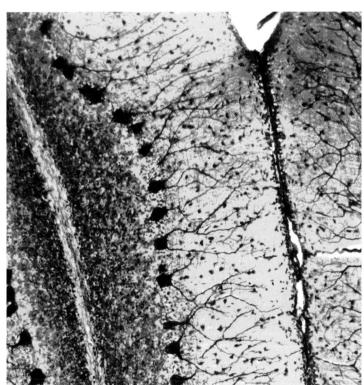

Left A very powerful microscope is needed to see neurons. Here you can see the cell body of a neuron with its wispy dendrites.

Above In this brain cross-section, the the black dots are the cell bodies of neurons, with their axons leading off to the right.

NEUROTRANSMITTERS

Nerve signals are constantly whizzing from neuron to neuron all around your body – yet no two neurons ever actually touch. Instead, there is a small gap between connecting neurons called a **synapse**. When a nerve signal is passed on from one neuron to the next, it is carried across the gap by special chemicals called **neurotransmitters**.

The chemicals are released by the neuron that is sending the signal. Droplets of neurotransmitters are stored inside the nerve-ending in tiny sacs called vesicles. When a nerve signal arrives at the nerve-ending, the vesicles drift towards the synapse and spill out their contents into the gap. The neurotransmitters flood across the gap and wash up against the other nerve.

Dendrites collect nerve signal from another neuron

Nerve signal passes along axon, or tail, of neuron

Right This enlarged view shows the synapse between two nerve endings (the two orange-yellow blobs). The red circles in the top nerve-ending are vesicles.

To pass to the next neuron, the signal must jump across the synapse

Left Inside every nerve ending are sacs of chemical transmitters. These are released into the synapse when the nerve is activated, or "excited," by a nerve signal. If the adjoining nerve has the right receptors, the signal will pass on.

Arrival of nerve signal triggers release of neurotransmitters

Neurotransmitters are stored in vesicles at end of dendrite

Neurotransmitter molecules flow out into synapse

Receptor sites accept the neurotransmitter molecules

BRAIN POWER!

- There are more than 40 different neurotransmitters.
- Noradrenaline helps to control heartbeat and blood flow.
- Dopamine works in the areas of the brain that control movement and coordination.
- Endorphins are used by the brain to control pain.
- Acetylcholine is involved in making muscles contract.

Sedatives

The vesicles in nerve endings store only a limited supply of neurotransmitter chemicals. Each time a transmitter is released into a synapse, the nerve ending must reabsorb it – otherwise it will quickly run out. Sedatives are medical drugs that reduce tension. Some sedatives work by blocking the reabsorption of neurotransmitters that keep you alert and active, slowing you down so that you relax.

Left When you wake up in the morning, it is because certain nerves are flooding your brain with the neurotransmitter serotonin – and any nerve that is receptive gets an alarm call!

Below When you're making a tricky move on a skateboard, your nerve endings are releasing lots of dopamine, a neurotransmitter that helps muscles move more easily.

Lock and key

Neurotransmitter chemicals work a bit like keys in locks. In this case, the "locks" are special receptor sites in the dendrites of the receiving neuron. These sites accept only one kind of chemical. For the nerve signal to pass on, the neurotransmitter must be the right chemical that fits, or "unlocks," the receptor site. If the neurotransmitter fits, it changes the chemistry of the receiving nerve's membrane (skin). This starts off the electrical changes that pass the signal along the length of the neuron.

Pass it on

Because a receptor site responds only to one type of neurotransmitter, an active nerve will pass on the signal only to neurons that have the right receptors – even though it is linked to many others. So different types of signal follow different routes through the body.

If every single nerve signal were passed on by every single synapse, you would simply be overwhelmed by nerve signals. This is why at some synapses the receiving neurons react by passing on the signal, but at others they react by blocking it. This is called excitation and inhibition.

SPINAL CONNECTIONS

The central nervous system (CNS) is the focus of your nervous system. It acts like the central processing unit of a computer, receiving information from the whole body, analysing it and then deciding on the appropriate response. At the base of the brain, nerves emerging from the brain stem feed into the little hollow that runs through all the bones of your spine, forming an "expressway" of nerves called the spinal cord that runs all the way down your back. It is the spinal cord that keeps your brain in touch with the rest of your body.

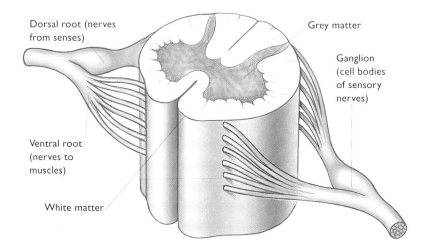

Dorsal root (nerves from senses)

Ventral root (nerves to muscles)

White matter

Grey matter

Ganglion (cell bodies of sensory nerves)

Left This infrared scan shows clearly how a thick bundle of nerves emerges from the base of the brain and leads down to the spinal cord, which runs down the back of the spine.

Above The spinal cord consists of a central, H-shaped core of grey matter (the cell bodies of neurons) surrounded by a tube of white matter (the axons, or tails, or neurons).

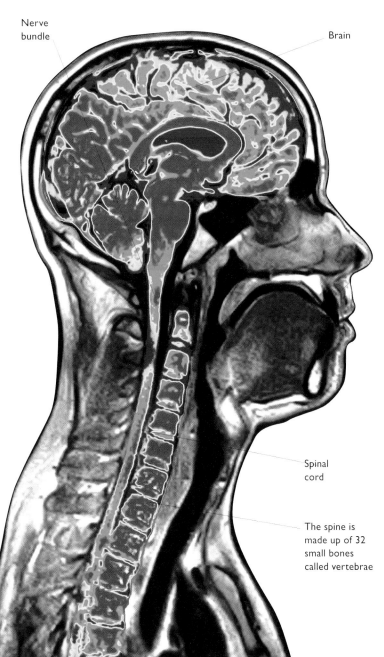

Nerve bundle

Brain

Spinal cord

The spine is made up of 32 small bones called vertebrae

When a message reaches it from the peripheral nervous system (PNS), the spinal cord always passes it on to the brain. But it is lot more than simply a message carrier: it can actually work without the brain, redirecting signals by itself to give instant body reactions called reflexes.

Inside the spinal cord

In an adult, the spinal cord is about 18 inches long and roughly the width of a finger. It consists of a whitish outer layer, called white matter, made up of long thin neuron tails packed tightly together. Within this is a core of grey matter – a pinkish-grey mass formed from the neuron's cell bodies. The spinal nerves of the PNS join the spinal cord at points called nerve roots.

The brain and spinal cord are surrounded by a cushioning bath of **cerebrospinal fluid**, or CSF, as well as three protective membranes (layers) called meninges – not to mention the encasing bones of the spine and skull. The CNS also needs a plentiful supply of blood to provide it with oxygen and nutrients.

Right Spinal nerves branch off the spinal cord in pairs, with one nerve on either side. There is a pair of nerves for each of the vertebrae (the individual bones of the spine) – all except the last one, called the tailbone. You have 32 vertebrae, so there are 31 pairs of nerves, arranged into four groups.

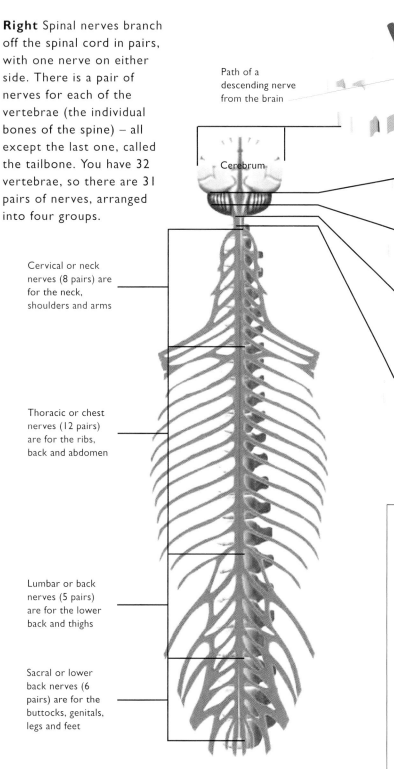

Path of a descending nerve from the brain

Cerebrum

Cortex

Mid-brain

Pons

Upper medulla

Lower medulla

Cervical or neck nerves (8 pairs) are for the neck, shoulders and arms

Thoracic or chest nerves (12 pairs) are for the ribs, back and abdomen

Lumbar or back nerves (5 pairs) are for the lower back and thighs

Sacral or lower back nerves (6 pairs) are for the buttocks, genitals, legs and feet

BRAIN POWER!

- The CNS sends out messages to over 600 different muscles.
- Around 100 million bits of data rush up the spinal cord each minute.
- To prevent information overload, 99% of the data from your spinal cord is filtered out by a part of the brain called the reticular formation.
- Of 43 nerves emerging from the CNS, 3 take in signals from the senses and 6 send out signals to the muscles, while the remaining 34 do both.
- The sciatic nerve gets its name from the Latin for "a pain in the thigh bone."

Spinal damage

One of the worst injuries a rider falling from a motorbike or horse can suffer is damage to the spine and spinal cord. Injury to the spine can cut off the brain's communication with the body, and the victim may lose both sensation and muscle power below the place where the cord is damaged. Injuries below the neck can cause paraplegia – weakness or paralysis below the waist. Injuries to the neck can cause quadriplegia – paralysis below the neck.

Up and down pathways

Nerve signals can only travel one way along a nerve. Some bundles of nerves – or "pathways" as they are known, take signals away from the senses and up to the brain. These are called ascending pathways. Nerve pathways called descending pathways take signals down from the brain to the body's muscles, giving them instructions to move.

REFLEX ACTION

There are two kinds of nerves in your body. First there are the sensory nerves that carry all the responses of your senses, from touch to sight, to your brain. Then there are the motor nerves that carry signals from your brain to your muscles, telling them to move. In most parts of your body, these two kinds of nerve run side by side. So the sensory nerve that sends back touch signals from your toes travels alongside the motor nerve that stimulates the muscles of your toes. But as these two kinds of nerve enter your spine, their paths diverge — and this provides your body with a very useful shortcut mechanism.

Quick reactions

If you accidentally touch a hot plate, even a fraction of a second's delay in removing your hand can result in a serious burn. Unfortunately, the time it takes for the signal to travel to your brain, and for your brain to process the signal and decide to pull your hand away from the plate, may not be short enough to avoid injury. This is where the split of the nerves entering your spinal cord proves useful, enabling you to make lightning-quick responses called **reflexes**.

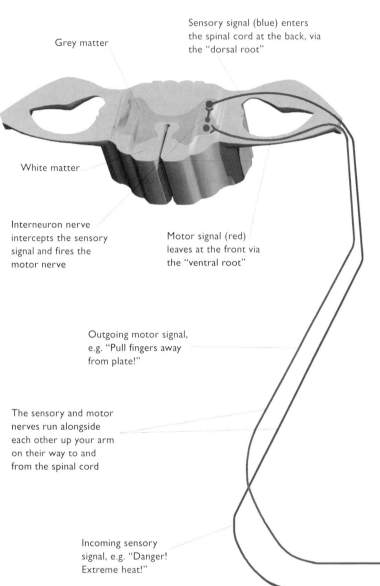

Grey matter

Sensory signal (blue) enters the spinal cord at the back, via the "dorsal root"

White matter

Interneuron nerve intercepts the sensory signal and fires the motor nerve

Motor signal (red) leaves at the front via the "ventral root"

Outgoing motor signal, e.g. "Pull fingers away from plate!"

The sensory and motor nerves run alongside each other up your arm on their way to and from the spinal cord

Incoming sensory signal, e.g. "Danger! Extreme heat!"

Above We can enjoy the warmth of a camp fire on a cold night. But automatic, unconscious reflex actions produced by the spine make us pull back instantly when the flames get dangerously hot.

Types of reflex

Inborn reflexes are those you were born with, such as shivering and urinating. One example is the knee-jerk, which makes your knee jerk sharply when someone taps the tendon just below your knee. Conditioned reflexes are those you acquire as you grow older by repeated practice. Doing the same thing again and again is habit-forming, as certain nerve pathways get reinforced by repeated use. This is conditioning, and it is how you learn to kick a football or play the piano without thinking.

Left If you had to think about how to move your fingers to play every single note, you could only bash out single notes on the piano. But practice reinforces nerve pathways and produces conditioned reflexes, so you can play faster and more smoothly without having to think about what you are doing.

Instant response

Reflexes are automatic reactions that you have little control over. They are so quick that you become aware of them only after they have happened. Most reflexes work by intercepting the signal sent by the sensory nerve where it enters the spine. This is done by a nerve cell called an interneuron, which makes a direct connection to the appropriate motor nerve. The interneuron automatically fires the motor nerve, producing an ultra-quick reaction, such as jerking your hand away from a hot plate.

Above Conditioning also helps you to get better at electronic games. The more you play, the faster your reactions get (up to a certain point), because your nervous system literally learns what to do, and cuts down your brain's thinking time to a minimum.

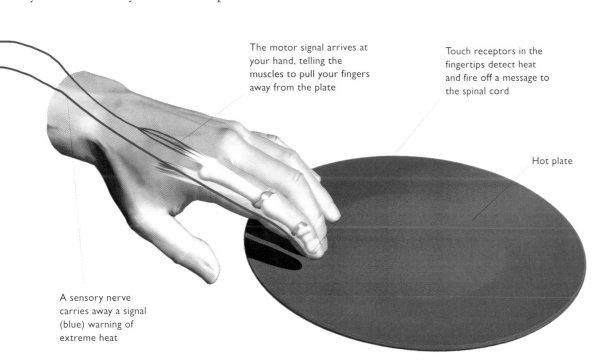

The motor signal arrives at your hand, telling the muscles to pull your fingers away from the plate

Touch receptors in the fingertips detect heat and fire off a message to the spinal cord

Hot plate

A sensory nerve carries away a signal (blue) warning of extreme heat

Left when you touch something painfully hot, sensory signals from your hand go to your spine and loop through the interneuron, which sends a signal straight back to pull your hand away.

BODY MAP

If someone taps you on the shoulder, you are instantly aware of exactly where and how hard you've been touched. How can this be? Well, you know how hard you've been touched from the rate at which nerve impulses reach your brain. And you know where the touch has occurred because your brain has its own "map" of the body.

This map of the body is called the sensory cortex, and it runs around the top of the brain's wrinkled outer surface, just as the band from a set of headphones runs across your head. Of course, it is not a real map. It is simply that different parts of the brain's cortex are dedicated to receiving nerve signals from specific parts of the body. Your brain can immediately pinpoint where a signal has come from by which part of the cortex starts to "buzz" when a nerve signal arrives and activates it.

Below Lips have a greater density of nerve endings than any other part of the body – not only sensory nerves that respond to touch, but also motor nerves that control movement. This makes kissing pleasurable, and it is one reason why we use kissing to show our affection for others.

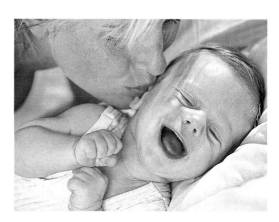

Sensitive areas

Just how much of the sensory cortex is devoted to each part of the body depends on how many nerve endings there are. A part of the body with plenty of nerve endings takes up a big part of the cortex; a part with only a few nerve endings gets just a little. Your face has more nerve endings than any other body part. Your lips, in particular, are jam-packed with them, which is why lips are so sensitive and kissing can be so exciting.

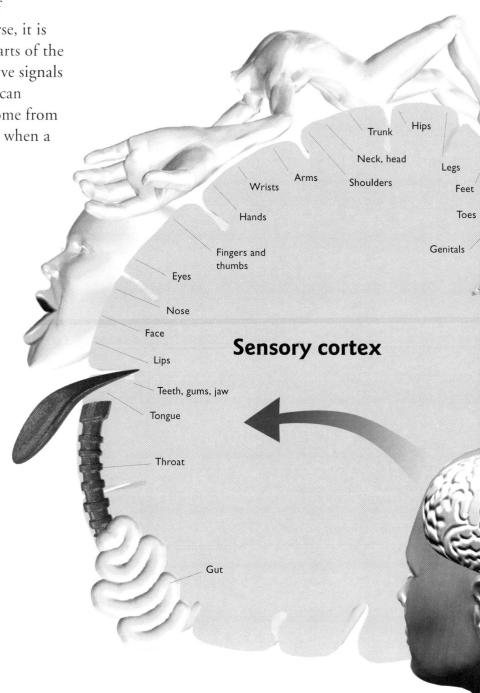

Trunk
Hips
Neck, head
Legs
Arms
Shoulders
Feet
Wrists
Toes
Hands
Fingers and thumbs
Genitals
Eyes
Nose
Face
Sensory cortex
Lips
Teeth, gums, jaw
Tongue
Throat
Gut

Your hands, too, have plenty of nerve endings, which is why we use our hands to feel with. In fact, over half the cortex is devoted to the hands and face. Some areas, such as your back, have relatively few nerve-endings, which is why they are allocated only a tiny part of the cortex.

Muscle map

Just behind the sensory cortex is another band called the motor cortex, which is is a map of your muscles and the motor nerves that trigger them. When you want to move in a certain way, the brain activates the appropriate parts of the motor cortex, which send out signals along the right motor nerves to make the right muscles work.

These "homunculus" (little man) diagrams show how different parts of the motor cortex and the sensory cortex control different parts of the body

Above Shaping clay to make a vase on a potter's wheel calls for great delicacy of touch. This brings into play the large area of the sensory cortex devoted to your hands' sense of touch, and the equally large area of your motor cortex devoted to controlling your hand movements.

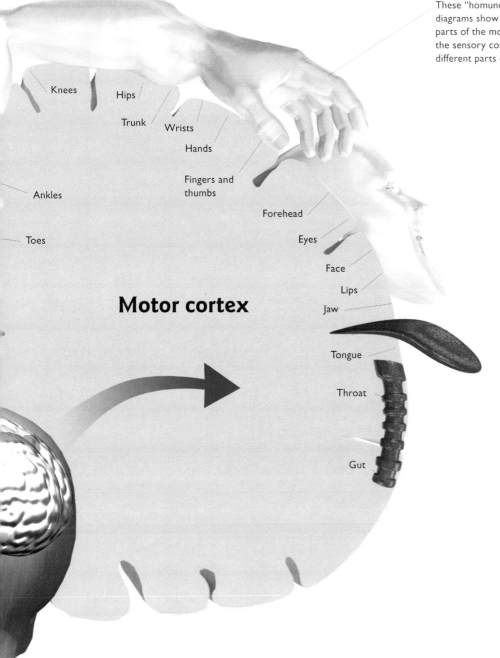

Knees

Hips

Trunk

Wrists

Hands

Fingers and thumbs

Ankles

Forehead

Toes

Eyes

Face

Lips

Motor cortex

Jaw

Tongue

Throat

Gut

Left The left half of this illustration shows the sensory cortex – the brain's map of sensory nerve-endings. The right half shows the areas of the motor cortex, the brain's map of motor nerves to the muscles. Notice that there are sensory nerves in the gut, which is why you can feel pain here, but there are no motor nerves, which is why you can't control its movements. On the other hand, there are motor nerves to the throat, so you can control swallowing, but there are very few sensory nerves, so you can't feel much there.

LEFT AND RIGHT

Your brain has two hemispheres, or halves, and at first sight it seems like they are completely identical. For a start, they both have the same squidgy-walnut appearance. But a close investigation reveals some surprising things about the two halves.

First of all, the left side of your brain is mostly linked not to the left side of your body, but to the right. And your brain's right side is mostly linked to the left side of your body. The nerves to each side of the body actually cross over at the top of the spinal cord. Many animals' nerves cross over in the same way.

The brain's two halves are linked by the corpus callosum and are always swapping data, but one half is always dominant and takes charge. If you're right-handed, like most people are, your dominant half is probably the left hemisphere, which controls your right side. If you're left-handed, the chances are it is your right hemisphere that is dominant.

Below Each half of the brain specializes in different tasks. In general, the right side deals with tasks that rely on analysis and reasoning, while the left side deals with tasks that rely more on **intuition**.

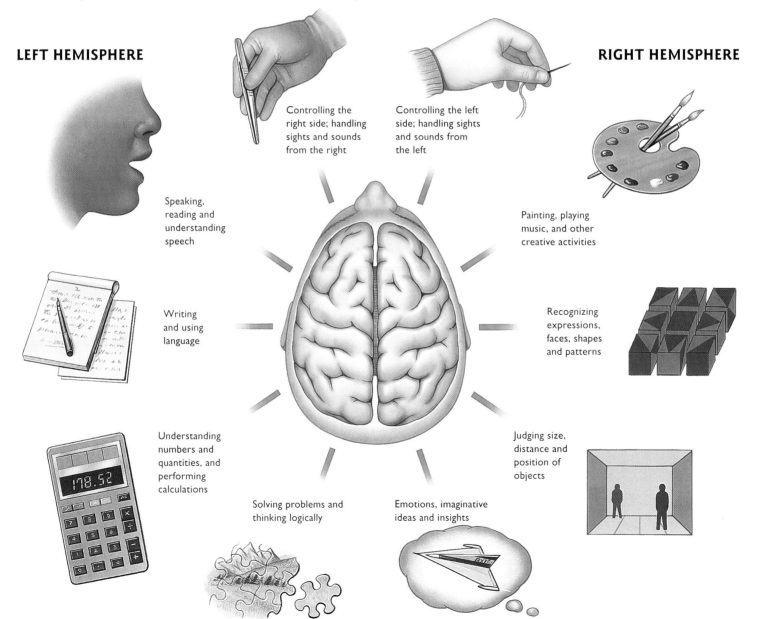

LEFT HEMISPHERE

Controlling the right side; handling sights and sounds from the right

Speaking, reading and understanding speech

Writing and using language

Understanding numbers and quantities, and performing calculations

Solving problems and thinking logically

RIGHT HEMISPHERE

Controlling the left side; handling sights and sounds from the left

Painting, playing music, and other creative activities

Recognizing expressions, faces, shapes and patterns

Judging size, distance and position of objects

Emotions, imaginative ideas and insights

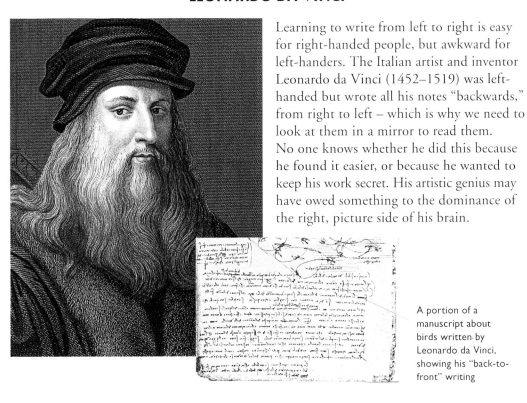

LEONARDO DA VINCI

Learning to write from left to right is easy for right-handed people, but awkward for left-handers. The Italian artist and inventor Leonardo da Vinci (1452–1519) was left-handed but wrote all his notes "backwards," from right to left – which is why we need to look at them in a mirror to read them. No one knows whether he did this because he found it easier, or because he wanted to keep his work secret. His artistic genius may have owed something to the dominance of the right, picture side of his brain.

A portion of a manuscript about birds written by Leonardo da Vinci, showing his "back-to-front" writing

BRAIN POWER!

- About 90% of people are right-handed.
- The remaining 10% are left-handed. Some are ambidextrous, meaning they can use both hands equally well.
- One-third of children born to two left-handed parents are left-handed themselves.
- A high proportion of identical twins are left-handed.
- One in five pairs of identical twins are different-handed.
- Around 90% of right-handers and 65% of left-handers have their speech center in the left side of the brain.

Words or pictures?

The second strange thing about the hemispheres is unique to humans: the two halves of our brains are not identical. While the sense areas on either side of the brain are like mirror images, some tasks are handled by one side only. In most people, the left side seems to be the "words" side, controlling the ability to speak, understand language and reason things out. The right side seems to be the "picture" side, specializing in tasks (such as drawing), giving you a sense of where things are and responding to intuition. Most activities involve a combination of these processes, so the two halves work together.

Left-handedness and great art

Interestingly, in a few left-handed people, word control seems to swap over to the right of the brain and picture control to the left. But this is not always so. In some left-handed people, the right side of the brain, their dominant side, remains the picture side. A few scientists think this may be why so many great artists in history have been left-handed.

Below In racket sports, left-handers sometimes have an advantage over right-handed players. This may be because the right, picture half of their brain is dominant. But it is more likely to be because they hit from angles that surprise right-handed opponents.

SEEING CLEARLY

Whenever you look at something, a tiny picture, just a fraction of an inch across, forms at the back of your eyes. The picture seems so big and clear that it probably never occurs to you that it is just a picture, like a picture taken by a camera. But your eyes are far superior to any camera. Some cameras may match the eye for sharpness, but none can focus on both a speck of dust and a distant star, and work in everything from dim starlight to bright sunshine.

Sitting in bony sockets in your skull, your eyes are little balls filled with a jelly-like substance called vitreous humor. At the front of each eye is a "glassy" outer layer called the cornea. This acts as a lens, bending light rays so that they enter your eye.

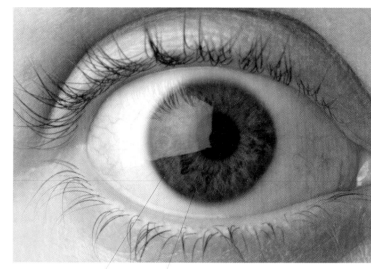

Iris   Pupil

Above Light enters your eye through the pupil. A muscular ring around the pupil, called the iris, widens or narrows to let in more or less light, depending on the conditions.

The sclera is the eye's tough but soft outer shell

The iris alters the size of the pupil

The pupil is the "window" that lets light into the eye

The cornea, the eye's main lens, projects the image into the eye

The lens helps to focus the picture inside the eye

Conjunctiva (protective mucous layer)

The light-sensitive retina lining detects light rays

The choroid is a blood-rich layer that nourishes the inside of the eye

Optic nerve leads to brain

Vitreous humor helps to give the eye its shape

Tiny muscles swivel the eye and move it up and down

Right The spherical structure of the eyeball, which measures about one inch across, can be seen in this cross-section.

The light rays enter through the dark hole called the pupil. They come together to form an image on the lining at the back of your eye called the retina. Another lens behind the pupil makes sure the picture is sharply focused. The retina is made up of millions of tiny light-sensitive cells. Whenever light hits one of these cells, it sends off a signal to the brain via a bundle of nerves called the optic nerve.

Color vision

Your retina has two types of light-sensitive cell, called rods and cones. Rods can detect anything from the brightest light to the dimmest, yet they cannot tell one color from another. So if you saw only with rods, you would see in black and white. It is cones that give color to your world.

There are three main kinds of cone: some are sensitive mostly to red light, some to green light and some to blue light. There may also be cones that are yellow-light sensitive. It used to be thought that the brain saw different colors simply by comparing the strength of the signals from each cone type. Scientists now think that colors may be further processed inside the brain, to analyse them in terms of two pairs of opposite colors: blue and yellow, and red and green.

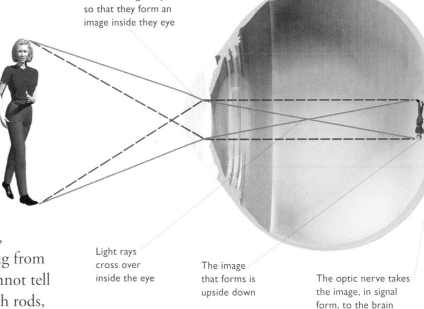

The cornea and lens both bend light rays so that they form an image inside they eye

Light rays cross over inside the eye

The image that forms is upside down

The optic nerve takes the image, in signal form, to the brain

Above The images that form in your eyes are upside down and back to front. Fortunately, your brain interprets the image signals it receives and shows you the world correctly: right-way-round and right-way-up.

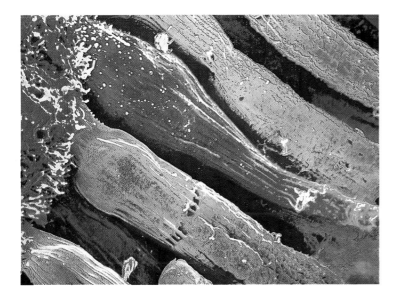

Above In this artificially colored electron microscope image of the retina, rod cells appear orange and cone cells appear blue. Rods greatly outnumber cone cells, in the ratio of about 18 to 1.

Eagle-eyed

A bald eagle's eye is packed with light sensitive cells

Human eyesight is very good compared with that of insects, which see everything as a blur, although they are very aware of movement. But we are quite short-sighted compared to birds of prey. An eagle's eyes, for example, are five times more densely packed with light-sensitive cells than our own. As a result, an eagle can spot a rabbit at a distance of 3 miles. Even the most keen-sighted human would have difficulty seeing a rabbit just half a mile away.

THE MIND'S EYE

Like a TV camera sending electrical signals along cables to form pictures on your TV screen, your eyes send nerve impulses along your optic nerves to form pictures in your visual cortex – your brain's very own "TV screen."

The retina, the layer at the back of your eye, is lined with light-sensitive cells arranged into groups. Whenever a group is hit by enough light, each cell sends a tiny electrical signal to a special relay cell called a bipolar cell. Straightaway, the bipolar cell passes on the signal to a cell called a ganglion cell, which processes information from this and other nearby bipolar cells. The axons of ganglion cells form the two optic nerves (*optic* simply means "of the eyes"). The optic nerves carry the results of all this information processing to the rest of the brain.

Optical traffic

Signals from all the many ganglions behind each eye whizz away down the optic nerves, like cars hurtling along a busy motorway. The two optic nerves meet at a crossroads in your head called the optic chiasma. At the crossroads, half of the signals from each eye go off to the right of the brain, and the other half go off to the left. So each half of your brain gets half the picture from each of your eyes.

Right in the middle of your brain is the signal sorting office, called the lateral geniculate nucleus, or LGN for short. The LGN starts to make sense of the signals, splitting them into different kinds of images – pictures showing movement, pictures showing dark and light, pictures showing lines, and so on. It sends each picture signal out in a different direction, down nerves called optic radiations.

Sitting next to the LGN is the brain's optical troubleshooter, the superior colliculus. This bundle of nerves is always on the watch for danger, checking

Above Inside your brain, a bundle of nerves called the superior colliculus is constantly monitoring the signals coming from your eyes. It makes you dodge instantly if your cycling partner suddenly swerves into your path.

Right To catch a baseball whizzing past like a rocket, a fielder needs to be certain where the ball is in the air and judge its distance accurately in a split second. This is made possible by the stereoscopic vision given by our two eyes.

the pictures for anything wrong or unusual. For example, if it spots a falling brick about to hit your head, it sends a warning signal to your brain so you can try to get out of the way.

All the different kinds of picture sent by the LGN arrive at the brain's visual cortex, which interprets them as a single image so you can see what's going on. Although it may be hard to believe, the entire process of seeing takes just a split second.

Stereoscopic vision

Each of your two eyes gives a slightly different view of the same object. The nearer the object is to you, the more different the view is from each eye. Your brain combines the two views to give an impression of three-dimensional depth and solidity. This is called stereoscopic vision, and it is crucial to judging distances. Try catching a ball with one eye shut and you'll see just what a difference it makes!

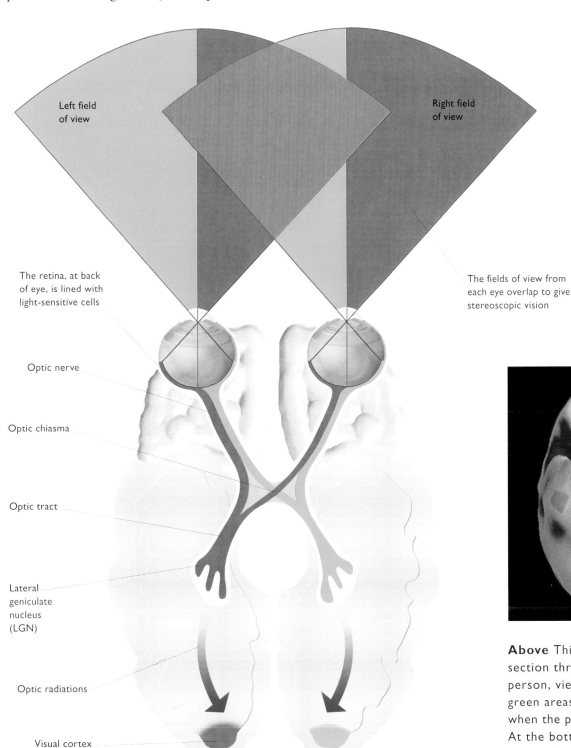

Left field of view

Right field of view

The retina, at back of eye, is lined with light-sensitive cells

The fields of view from each eye overlap to give stereoscopic vision

Optic nerve

Optic chiasma

Optic tract

Lateral geniculate nucleus (LGN)

Optic radiations

Visual cortex

Left Nerve signals produced by the light-sensitive cells of your retinas are sent along the optic nerves to the visual cortex at the back of your brain. At the optic chiasma, signals from the left side of each retina join up, as do those from the right side.

Above This electronic scan is a cross-section through the brain of a living person, viewed from above. The red and green areas show activity in the brain when the person is looking at something. At the bottom of the picture is the visual cortex, in the brain's occipital lobe.

SOUND SENSE

Sounds are made up of tiny vibrations in the air, and your ears are devices for picking up these vibrations. The flap on the side of your head, the visible part of the ear, is merely the entrance to the real workings of your ear – the incredibly sensitive vibration-detectors that lie inside your head. The ear flap is specially shaped to channel sounds into a tunnel called the ear canal. To keep out dirt and insects, the tunnel is lined with hairs and covered in an amber wax released by glands in the tunnel wall.

The drum in your ear

A little way inside the tunnel, in what is called your middle ear, sound hits a thin wall of skin called the eardrum, causing it to vibrate. High-pitched sounds vibrate the eardrum rapidly, while low-pitched sounds vibrate it slowly. Most sounds are a complex mix of fast and slow vibrations.

The eardrum touches the ossicles – three linked bones that form the ear's "amplifier." The three bones are all known by latin names: the *malleus*, or hammer, the *incus*, or anvil, and the *stapes*, or stirrup.

Below When you pluck a guitar, the strings vibrate. The vibrating strings send ripples of vibration through the air, which reach your ears as sound.

Right This cross-section shows the workings of the ear, from the outer flap to the tubes of the inner ear and the nerve that takes sound signals to the brain.

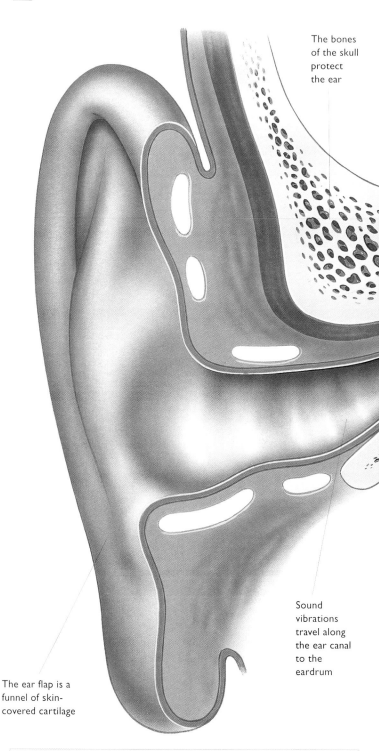

The bones of the skull protect the ear

Sound vibrations travel along the ear canal to the eardrum

The ear flap is a funnel of skin-covered cartilage

BRAIN POWER!

- Pitch is measured in Hertz (Hz), or vibrations per second.
- Humans can hear sounds between 20 Hz and 20,000 Hz.
- A dog can hear sounds between 15 Hz and 50,000 Hz.
- A bat can hear and make sounds as high as 120,000 Hz.
- Dolphins may be able to hear sounds higher than 150,000 Hz.

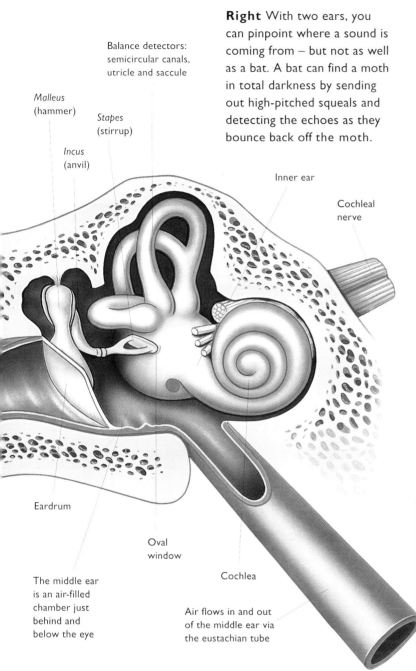

Balance detectors: semicircular canals, utricle and saccule

Malleus (hammer)

Stapes (stirrup)

Incus (anvil)

Inner ear

Cochleal nerve

Eardrum

Oval window

Cochlea

The middle ear is an air-filled chamber just behind and below the eye

Air flows in and out of the middle ear via the eustachian tube

Right With two ears, you can pinpoint where a sound is coming from – but not as well as a bat. A bat can find a moth in total darkness by sending out high-pitched squeals and detecting the echoes as they bounce back off the moth.

Beyond the oval window is the cochlea, a winding set of three tubes that looks a bit like snail's shell. In the middle tube is the Organ of Corti, where sounds are picked up. It contains rows of fine hairs covered by a flap. Pressure waves moving through the fluid inside the cochlea wash over the flap, making it wave up and down. The flap's motion tugs on the hairs, like fingers on harp strings. The wiggling hairs send signals to the brain via the cochleal nerve, and you hear the sound.

When sound vibrates the eardrum, it rattles the hammer against the anvil. The anvil, in turn, shakes the stirrup. Because the hammer is the biggest of the three bones, it moves a long way with each vibration. The stirrup is the smallest and vibrates only a little way, but each vibration is much stronger.

The vibrating stirrup batters a tough membrane called the oval window, which forms the entrance to the inner ear. The oval window is 30 times smaller than the eardrum, and this has the effect of concentrating the vibrations so that they become even more intense. As the oval window vibrates, it sends waves of pressure through the delicate, fluid-filled parts of the inner ear.

Balancing act

Even with your eyes shut, you can still tell if you are bending over or leaning to one side. This is because you have balance detectors inside your inner ear. The ear's balance detectors are three linked tubes called semicircular canals and two cavities called the utricle and saccule. All are fluid-filled and work a bit like a spirit level. When you tilt or swivel your head, the fluid lags behind a little, pulling on tiny hairs that detect the movement and send messages to your brain.

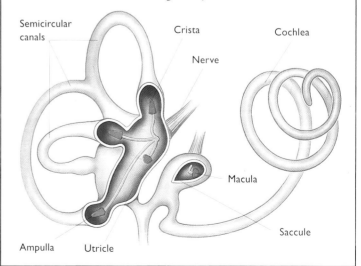

Semicircular canals

Crista

Cochlea

Nerve

Macula

Saccule

Ampulla

Utricle

SMELL AND TASTE

Without your senses of smell and taste, eating would be a bit of a chore. Flavor is the combination of smell and taste that makes your food enjoyable. You are usually not aware of the link between the two, until you get a cold and realize that your blocked-up nose has helped to rob your food of its flavor!

Your nose can detect a smell by picking up just a few molecules of a substance in the air. It can tell the difference between over 3,000 different substances.

Your sense of taste seems more vague, and the detectors on your tongue can only tell you the difference between four main types of taste. But when you eat, you experience other sensations as well as smell and taste, such as heat and cold, texture, and appearance. All these mean you have no problem telling one kind of apple from another or brown bread from white. Bad smells and unpleasant tastes often act as warning signals, telling us that something we are about to eat may be harmful.

Below When you smell a flower, the air carries small molecules given off by the flower to the olfactory epithelium. The scent molecules are identified by smell receptors in the olfactory epithelium.

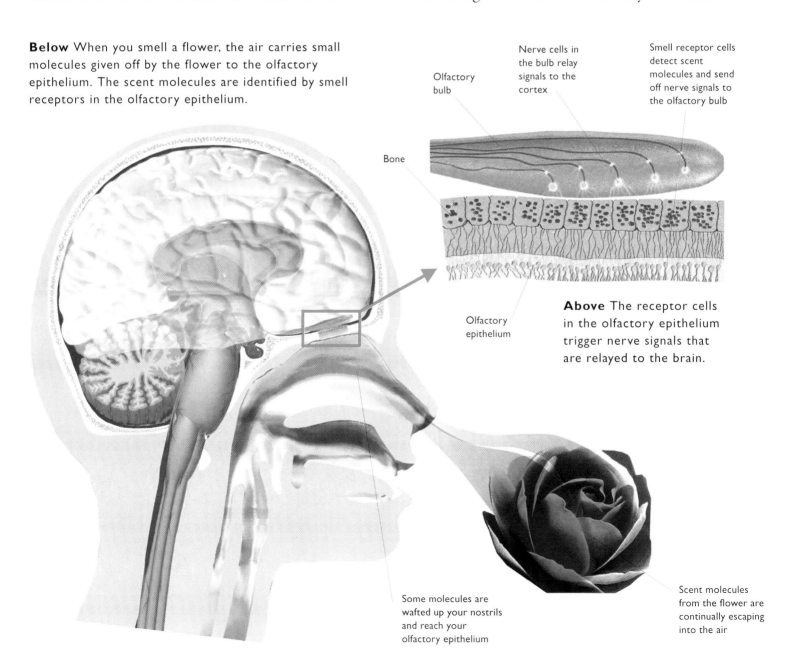

Olfactory bulb

Nerve cells in the bulb relay signals to the cortex

Smell receptor cells detect scent molecules and send off nerve signals to the olfactory bulb

Bone

Olfactory epithelium

Above The receptor cells in the olfactory epithelium trigger nerve signals that are relayed to the brain.

Some molecules are wafted up your nostrils and reach your olfactory epithelium

Scent molecules from the flower are continually escaping into the air

Below There are four types of taste bud – sweet, salty, sour, and bitter. Each one is concentrated in a different place on the tongue. So you detect certain tastes more strongly on one part of your tongue than another.

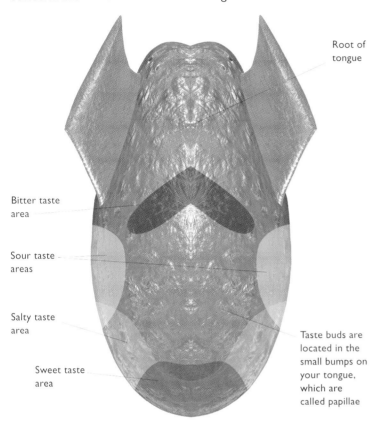

Root of tongue

Bitter taste area

Sour taste areas

Salty taste area

Sweet taste area

Taste buds are located in the small bumps on your tongue, which are called papillae

On the tip of your tongue

Your taste receptors are your tongue's taste buds. If you stick your tongue out and look at it in a mirror, you will see little nobbles all over its surface. These nobbles are called papillae and each one contains 100–200 taste buds.

To reach the buds and set off the tiny detector hairs they contain, food must first dissolve in saliva – which is why you can't taste things that don't easily dissolve, such as a plastic beaker. There are four kinds of bud, each responding to a different taste: sweet, salty, sour and bitter. Some areas of your tongue have more of one kind than others. The tip has lots of sweet buds, while salty tastes set off the taste buds just behind the tip. The side of your tongue has lots of sour buds. Bitter tastes are picked up really strongly right at the back of your tongue.

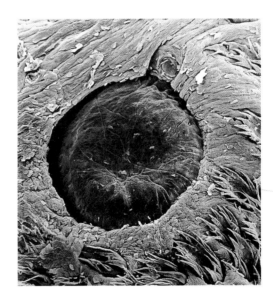

Left This electron-microscope image shows a single papilla on the surface of the tongue.

The taste buds in this papilla, called a papilla vallata, are sensitive to bitter tastes

Getting up your nose

You smell things with a tiny patch of cells inside the top of your nose called the olfactory epithelium. ("Olfactory" is the technical word for things to do with smell.) The epithelium is only postage-stamp size, yet it is packed with over 10 million receptor cells, each with 20 or so scent-detecting hairs called cilia. As you breathe in, molecules of a substance waft up your nose and land on the epithelium, where they dissolve in its mucus covering and stick onto the cilia. The cilia send signals to a cluster of nerve cells called the olfactory bulb, which relay them to your brain.

Below A cross-section of a papilla showing the taste buds. Each bud contains cells with tiny hairs called microvilli. Saliva containing dissolved food washes over the bud. If the saliva contains the right taste, the hairs act like triggers and cause the cell to fire off nerve signals.

Surface of papilla

Taste buds line the walls of the crevice

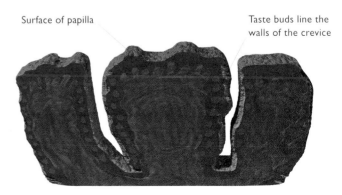

BRAIN POWER!

- Dogs can pick up scents 10,000 times fainter than humans can.
- By age 20, you have lost 20% of your sense of smell.
- By age 60, you have 60% of your sense of smell.
- In total, there are 10,000 taste buds on your tongue.
- A baby has taste buds all over its mouth, not just on its tongue.

FEELING TOUCHED

The sensations of sight, hearing, smell and taste are picked up in just one or two places about your body. But touch is spread all over your body, from head to toe, because your touch receptors are located in the skin. Some parts, such as your face, have more touch receptors than others, such as the small of your back, so they are more sensitive. As well as touch and pressure, these receptors can also detect pain, heat and cold.

Below This picture shows a section of skin, about 1/20 inch thick, with some of the main different kinds of touch receptor.

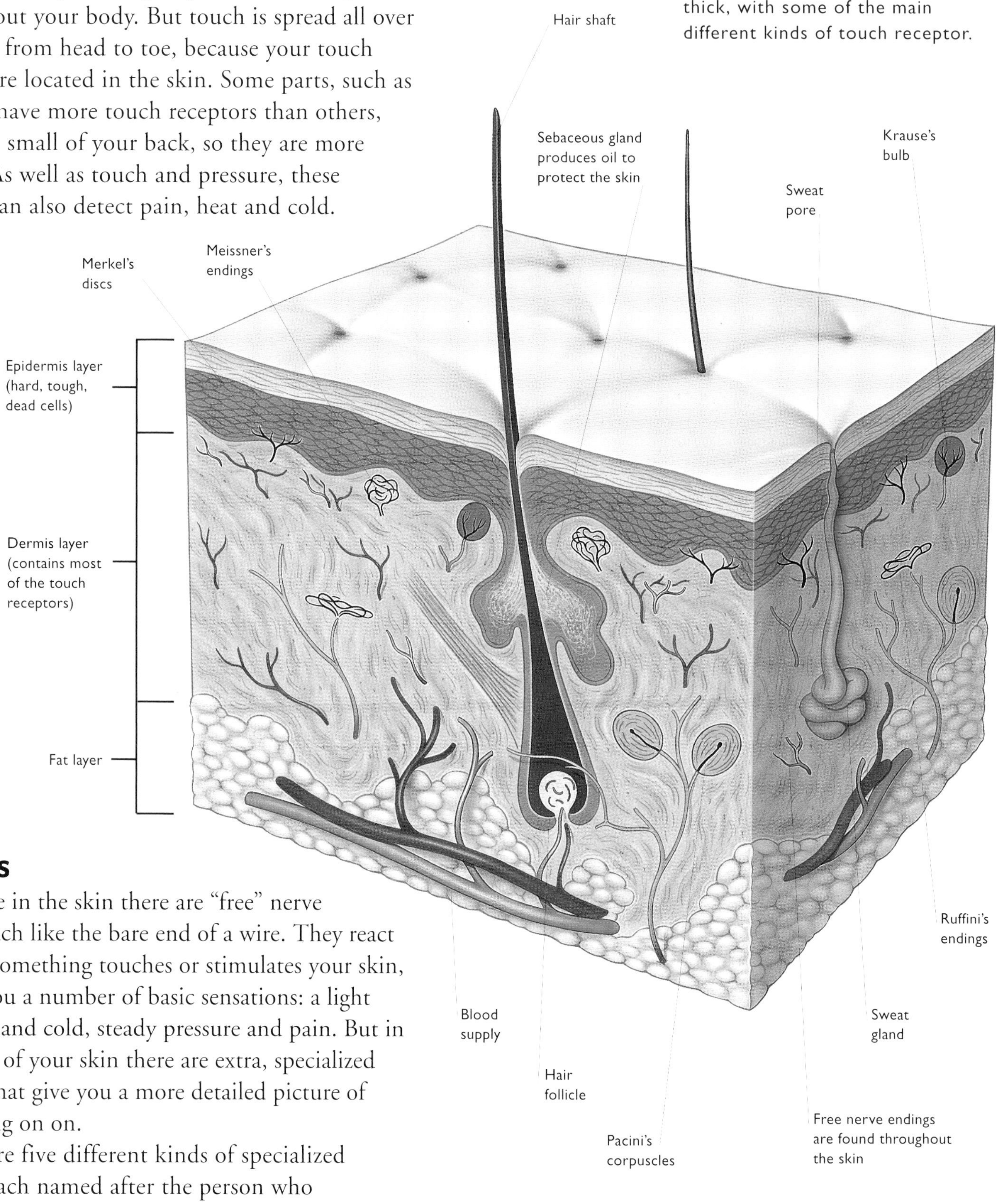

Hair shaft

Sebaceous gland produces oil to protect the skin

Krause's bulb

Sweat pore

Merkel's discs

Meissner's endings

Epidermis layer (hard, tough, dead cells)

Dermis layer (contains most of the touch receptors)

Fat layer

Ruffini's endings

Sweat gland

Blood supply

Hair follicle

Pacini's corpuscles

Free nerve endings are found throughout the skin

Feelings

Everywhere in the skin there are "free" nerve endings, each like the bare end of a wire. They react whenever something touches or stimulates your skin, and give you a number of basic sensations: a light touch, hot and cold, steady pressure and pain. But in some parts of your skin there are extra, specialized receptors that give you a more detailed picture of what's going on on.

There are five different kinds of specialized receptor, each named after the person who discovered it. Two of them, Meissner's endings and

Pacini's corpuscles, are ultra-sensitive and react when your skin is touched suddenly, even by the briefest of contacts. It may be this response that helps you distinguish delicate textures by touch alone, such as the difference between cotton and linen.

The other three specialized cells are Krause's bulbs, Ruffini's endings, and Merkel's discs, and they seem to respond not to a sudden touch but to steady pressure. Krause's bulbs and Ruffini's endings can detect temperature. Ruffini's endings and Pacini's corpuscles can also detect vibrations.

Aches and pains

Pain receptors set off alarm bells when there is damage to the body or the likelihood of damage. Nerve signals fired off by the receptors can take one of two pathways to the brain: a fast track that helps you avoid further damage, and a slower track that acts as a reminder to your brain that the damage is still there.

Above: Some kinds of touch, such as stroking a dog or a cat, are especially pleasant. Meissner's endings, found mostly in the fingertips, probably play most part in this.

Right When you're out in a bitter wind, receptors in your skin detect cold and set off a shivering reflex that generates heat by rapidly contracting and relaxing your muscles.

How hot or heavy?

When any of the different touch receptors in your skin is stimulated, it fires off nerve signals to your brain. The rate at which the nerve signals are fired off tells your brain, for example, just how hot things are or just how lightly you have been touched. But the receptors do not go on firing forever, and the rate of firing soon slows down no matter how strong the touch or sensation is. Once your brain has been told, the receptor sends only an occasional reminder. This is why you stop feeling your clothes soon after you put them on in the morning.

SPEAK AND UNDERSTAND

Speaking is one of our many unique talents. Some other animals, such as dolphins, can communicate with a range of different sounds, but none uses anything remotely similar to human speech.

When someone speaks to you, your ears pick up the sound and feed nerve signals to your brain. Your brain then translates the sound signal into meaningful words. Although you think that you can hear gaps between the words of a normally spoken sentence, analysis of human speech shows there are really no such gaps. The brain builds up words from the way the sounds run together. Experiments have shown that if you replace part of a word in a sentence with a mechanical click, you will hear that part of a word as if it has actually been said.

Learning to speak

Although you can make enough sound to wail and cry from the moment you are born, you cannot speak. But you quickly learn how during your first few years. Studies have shown that you are born with a built-in understanding of how sentences work. You then gradually learn how to fit the words you hear into place.

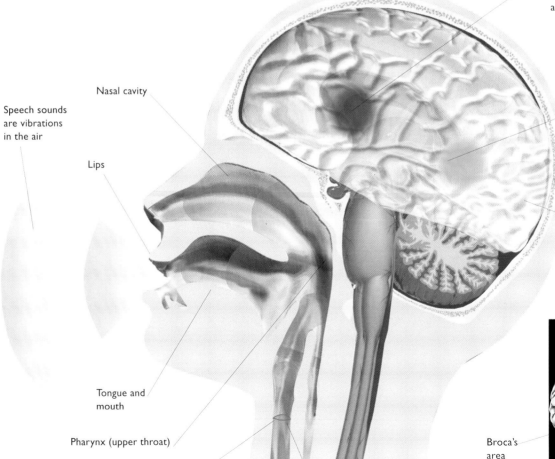

When Broca's area gets instructions to say something from Wernicke's area, it coordinates the movement of the vocal cords, lips, tongue and throat

Anything to do with words, whether it is speech that you hear or words that you read, is passed on to Wernicke's area, where you work out the meaning

Occipital lobe is used in reading

Speech sounds are vibrations in the air

Nasal cavity

Lips

Tongue and mouth

Pharynx (upper throat)

Broca's area

The vocal cords can only make simple "aaah" sounds – you change the sounds into words by altering the shape of your pharynx, tongue, lips, and mouth

Air from the lungs passes over bands of muscle called vocal cords, which vibrate and produce sounds

Above This false-colour scan of a person's brain during speech shows activity in Broca's area (yellow, red and white).

Finding the words

In the 19th century, a German **neurologist** Carl Wernicke (1848–1905) discovered that people whose brains had been damaged in a particular part of the cortex couldn't understand anything being said to them, or string a sentence or a few words together, even though they had no trouble making the right sounds. Wernicke realized it must be in this area of your brain, now called Wernicke's area, that you decide what you are going to say – and understand what others say to you. In recent years, brain scans have shown this to be true, but a slightly bigger area of the brain is involved than Wernicke thought. This area is better developed in girls' brains than boys'.

Making the sounds

Deciding what to say and actually making the sound are two different processes. The first scientists call language; the second they call speech. While language is made in Wernicke's area, a different area of the brain is involved in speech. This is called Broca's area, after its discoverer, the French surgeon Paule Pierre Broca (1824–80). Your brain first creates the sentence in Wernicke's area, and then sends the speech signal to Broca's area, which tells your tongue and vocal cords what to do.

Above When you read, the shape of the letters and words is analyzed in an area at the back of the brain's cortex called the occipital lobe.

Below These excited sports fans use different areas of their brains to shout than they do to understand what their companions are saying.

REMEMBER, REMEMBER

I f anyone tells you that your memory is hopeless, don't believe them! The human brain has an astounding ability to remember things – and your brain is no exception. Like all of us, you can remember thousands of words, details of faces, and all kinds of complex tasks. How can you do this?

There are billions of neurons in the brain, each one capable of connecting with over 1,000 others. When you remember something, your brain probably does it by creating a new pathway of nerve connections, called a memory trace. You probably forget things as the connections break down through lack of use.

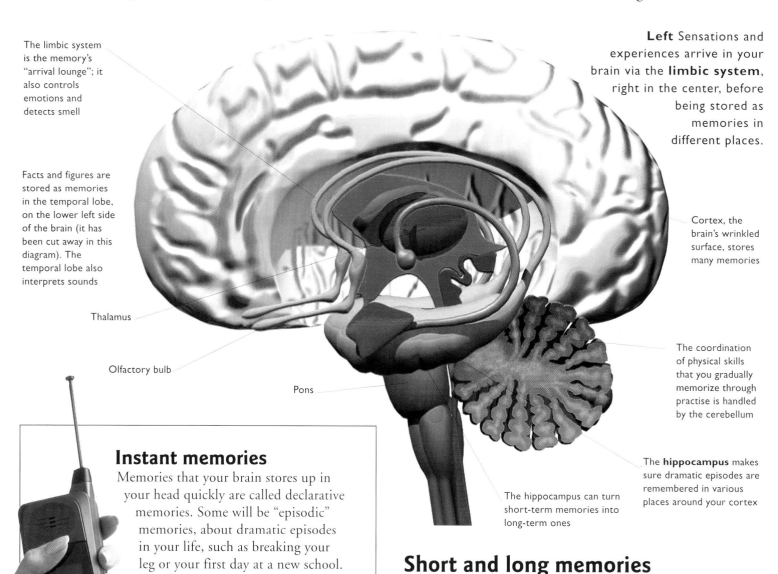

The limbic system is the memory's "arrival lounge"; it also controls emotions and detects smell

Facts and figures are stored as memories in the temporal lobe, on the lower left side of the brain (it has been cut away in this diagram). The temporal lobe also interprets sounds

Thalamus

Olfactory bulb

Pons

Left Sensations and experiences arrive in your brain via the **limbic system**, right in the center, before being stored as memories in different places.

Cortex, the brain's wrinkled surface, stores many memories

The coordination of physical skills that you gradually memorize through practise is handled by the cerebellum

The **hippocampus** makes sure dramatic episodes are remembered in various places around your cortex

The hippocampus can turn short-term memories into long-term ones

Instant memories

Memories that your brain stores up in your head quickly are called declarative memories. Some will be "episodic" memories, about dramatic episodes in your life, such as breaking your leg or your first day at a new school. You don't just remember a single fact, but also much of what you felt, saw, and said at the time. Facts, such as telephone numbers, dates and so on, are called "semantic" memories. Your brain seems to store these in the temporal lobe on the left side of your brain.

Short and long memories

You have three types of memory. First, there is sensory memory, which enables you to go on seeing, hearing or feeling something for a little while after it stops. You can write your name in the air with a sparkler firework because, if you're quick enough, you will be writing the last letter while your eyes are still seeing the first.

Secondly, you have what scientists call short-term memory, which is when your brain stores things for only a few seconds or minutes. This is what you use when you look up a number in the telephone book and remember it just long enough to dial. Your short term memory briefly stores most, if not all, of the things you experience.

Thirdly, you have long-term memory, which can last for months, years or even all your life. Long-term memory stores only selected information, such as important birthdays, names and addresses, and key events in your life.

Storing memories

Scientists studying memory have discovered that your brain stores memories in two main ways. They call these declarative and non-declarative memories.

Non-declarative memories are skills you have to teach your body by practicing them over and over again, such as playing football or the piano. Memories like this are stored in the strengthening of certain nerve connections throughout the body – not just in your brain. These connections are activated by part of the brain called the cerebellum.

Declarative memories are things you can store in your head alone and only have to experience once or a few times to memorize (see box on page 38). These memories are sent by the part of the brain called the hippocampus to be stored in the right place in the cortex, the brain's wrinkly rind.

Below Skills such as playing football you teach your body by practicing over and over again, so that the right nerve connections are slowly reinforced. These skills are stored as non-declarative memories.

Above A dramatic event, such as your wedding, forges strong nerve connections throughout the brain and is stored as a declarative memory. In later years, you may be able to recall every sensation you had on the day.

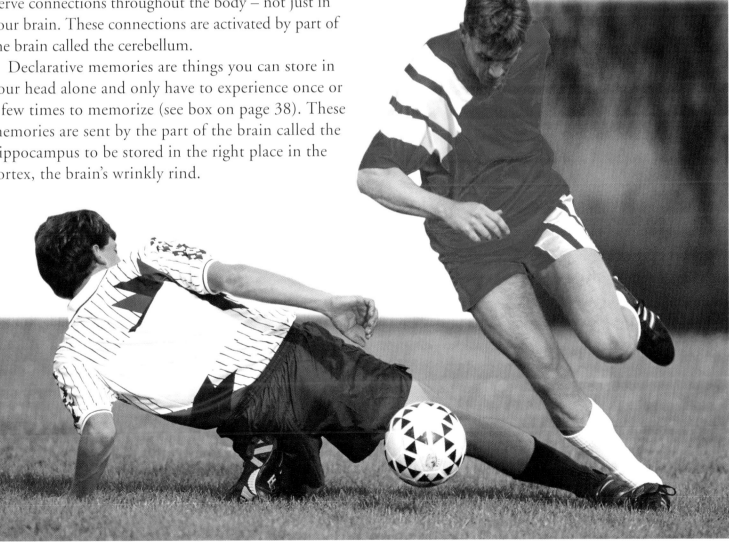

SWEET DREAMS

You will probably spend a third of your life asleep! Scientists know that sleep is essential to the human body, but they aren't sure exactly why. Your body carries on working while you sleep: your heart continues to beat, your lungs go on breathing, your food still gets digested. Even your brain remains active. What does seem to be different is the way your brain functions during sleep.

Brain waves

The tiny electrical signal that a brain cell produces when it fires off a nerve impulse is very difficult to detect. But scientists can measure bursts of electricity from all your brain cells combined with a sensitive electronic device called an electroencephalograph, or EEG. Electrodes attached to the head record the brain's electrical activity and display it as a wavy line on a screen or printed out on a graph.

Above and left EEGs are used in experiments to monitor brain activity during sleep. They display brain waves on a screen.

EEGs show that when you are awake, the brain is constantly buzzing, with so many cells firing off at once that there is no real pattern. But as you start to feel drowsy, brain cells begin to fire in a more coordinated way, and regular pulses of electrical activity, known as alpha waves, sweep across your brain every tenth of a second or so. Slower pulses called theta waves soon begin to appear too.

When you fall asleep, your breathing and brain waves become more regular. This is stage 1 sleep. After a few minutes, you enter into stage 2 sleep, and the waves become stronger and more rapid. Over the next 90 minutes, you fall more and more deeply asleep. In stages 3 and 4, the waves become stronger until the whole brain seems to throb gently once or twice a second, with the cortex ticking over quietly.

Right This graph shows how periods of shallow, dreaming sleep – called REM sleep – are interspersed with periods of deeper, non-dreaming sleep. You remember only your last dream, even though you may have had a series of many different dreams throughout the night.

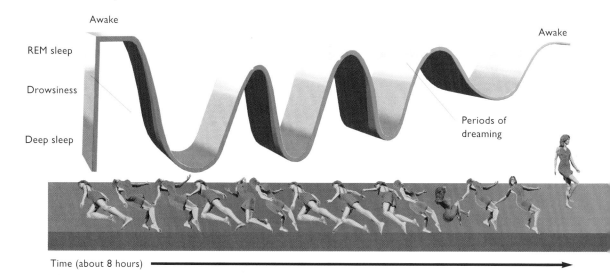

Awake

REM sleep

Drowsiness

Deep sleep

Awake

Periods of dreaming

Time (about 8 hours)

Dreaming

Suddenly, your body starts to fidget, your breathing becomes irregular and your brain starts to buzz with activity and nerve cells start to fire off all the time – and yet you are still fast asleep. What's more, your eyes begin to flick rapidly from side to side under their lids. This is called rapid eye movement, or REM.

BRAIN POWER!

- Your body may do routine body repairs during sleep.
- A prolonged lack of sleep can eventually kill a person.
- A new-born baby needs 18–20 hours of sleep each day.
- Most adults sleep for 7–8 hours each day.
- Sleepwalking occurs in periods of non-REM sleep.

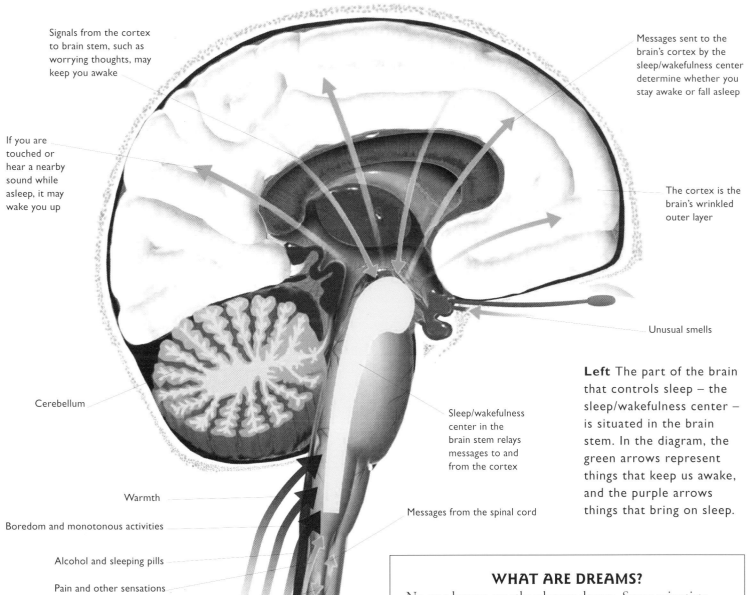

Signals from the cortex to brain stem, such as worrying thoughts, may keep you awake

If you are touched or hear a nearby sound while asleep, it may wake you up

Cerebellum

Warmth

Boredom and monotonous activities

Alcohol and sleeping pills

Pain and other sensations

Messages to the spinal cord

Messages sent to the brain's cortex by the sleep/wakefulness center determine whether you stay awake or fall asleep

The cortex is the brain's wrinkled outer layer

Unusual smells

Sleep/wakefulness center in the brain stem relays messages to and from the cortex

Messages from the spinal cord

Left The part of the brain that controls sleep – the sleep/wakefulness center – is situated in the brain stem. In the diagram, the green arrows represent things that keep us awake, and the purple arrows things that bring on sleep.

Most scientists think that when you have REM, you are dreaming. Throughout the night, periods of REM sleep lasting about 30 minutes or so seem to alternate with periods of deeper, steadier sleep. These periods of non-REM sleep get gradually shallower and shorter until finally you wake up.

WHAT ARE DREAMS?

No one knows exactly why we dream. Some scientists believe that dreaming is your brain's way of sorting out the previous day's experiences. During the day, your cortex is busy interpreting all the data coming in from your senses. But when you're asleep, the cortex tries to link up new experiences with old memories. Others believe that dreams are more significant and reveal truths about your subconscious mind. Sigmund Freud, the 19th-century Austrian doctor, suggested that dreams are your brain's way of expressing your deepest desires.

BRAIN PROBLEMS

Left Everyone gets sad sometimes, but people of all ages can suffer from depression. This is when sadness is not just a passing feeling but becomes a permanent state. If so, they may need medical help.

And no one would think it strange if you waved your arms wildly at school if you won the lottery. But they might think it odd if you did it every day for no reason.

Physical problems

If a person does start to behave abnormally, the cause could be "organic" – that is, it could be because there is something physically wrong with their nervous system. It may have been damaged, possibly by a bang on the head, too much alcohol, a brain tumor or diseases such as Parkinson's or Alzheimer's. Alternatively, the problem may be one they were born with.

Every now and then, we all feel sad, anxious or confused. Every now and then, we all escape into fantasy worlds, such as daydreaming, losing ourselves in books or watching TV. Every now and then, we all behave oddly, doing something in the wrong place or at the wrong time. But if this behavior becomes extreme, it may be a sign of illness.

Below The stress of taking exams can make anyone anxious or depressed. Sometimes, though, anxiety can become so extreme that students become ill.

Behaving oddly

It is impossible for anyone else to decide how another person is feeling, so when someone is upset mentally, doctors look for signs of strange behavior. But it is hard to decide just what kind of behavior is strange. It would be very strange to shout and wave your legs and arms wildly in classes at school, but it could be quite acceptable at a party.

BRAIN POWER!

- Meningitis is a condition in which the brain's protective layers, or meninges, become infected by germs and swollen.
- Alzheimer's disease occurs when the brain's neuron connections get disrupted by a build up of a protein called amyloid.
- A stroke occurs when a blood vessel supplying the brain becomes blocked.
- Parkinson's disease is a result of a deficiency of the neurotransmitter dopamine.

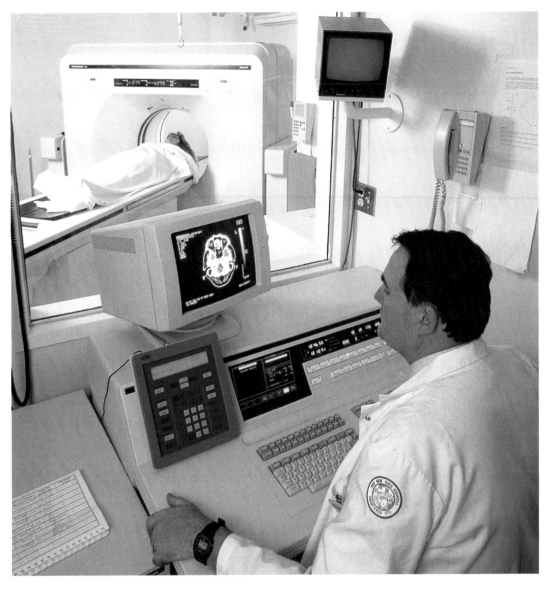

Right Modern scanning equipment produces images of slices through the brain, making it easier to spot if the cause of abnormal behavior is physical damage to the brain or part of the nervous system.

Neuroses and psychoses

People sometimes start behaving abnormally when there is no obvious physical cause. This does not mean that the problem is any less real. Indeed, many such problems often have real physical side-effects. But it is much harder for doctors to decide how to treat the problem. Problems like these are of two kinds: neuroses and psychoses.

A neurosis is when someone becomes abnormally anxious and worried. A phobia – an unusually strong fear of something, is a type of neurosis. For example, claustrophobia is when someone becomes very upset in small, enclosed spaces. A psychosis is when someone becomes so upset that they begin to lose touch with the real world. Someone who suffers from the psychosis of manic-depression swings from extreme happiness to extreme depression.

Treatments

There are many different ways of treating mental illness. Physical treatments involve surgery or giving people drugs that either repair damage to the nervous system or change the way it works to make them feel better. Therapy involves helping people talk through their problems and analyzing the way they think.

Psychoactive drugs

Psychoactive drugs alter the brain's chemistry and change the way you feel or behave – often by interfering with or mimicking neurotransmitters. They include caffeine in coffee, which excites the nervous system and makes you feel more alert, but also more anxious. Illegal drugs such as cocaine and ecstasy can excite the nervous system to a dangerous extent. Many psychoactive drugs are addictive.

BRAIN TEASERS

Can you select the right answers to these questions? (They are all in the book.) To check if you are correct, see the end of the quiz.

1 *What is a nerve?*
a   A bundle of nerve cells
b   A muscle in your leg
c   A kind of blood vessel

2 *Roughly how many neurons are there in your brain?*
a   15,000
b   15,000,000
c   15,000,000,000

3 *Which nerve carries signals from your eyes to your brain?*
a   The optic nerve
b   The vagus nerve
c   The sciatic nerve

4 *What are the gaps between nerves called?*
a   Bridges
b   Connectors
c   Synapses

5 *What percentage of people are left-handed?*
a   1%
b   10%
c   20%

6 *Which of these muscles can you move deliberately?*
a   Heart muscles
b   Gut muscles
c   Leg muscles

7 *What does your cerebellum control?*
a   Speaking
b   Balance and coordination
c   Memory

8 *What is a nerve that tells the muscles to move called?*
a   A muscle nerve
b   A motor nerve
c   A sensory nerve

9 *How many nerves branch off your spine?*
a   3
b   15
c   31

10 *How many cranial nerves do you have?*
a   120
b   29
c   12

11 *Which animals have the biggest brain?*
a   Humans
b   Gorillas
c   Whales

12 *What do the letters CNS stand for?*
a   Cerebral nerve synapse
b   Central nervous system
c   Combined nodal senses

13 *How many different tastes can your tongue distinguish?*
a   4
b   74
c   3,000

14 *Which of side of the brain controls your right hand?*
a   Right
b   Left
c   Neither

Answers: 1 a, 2 c, 3 a, 4 c, 5 b, 6 c, 7 b, 8 b, 9 c, 10 c, 11 c, 12 b, 13 a, 14 b

GLOSSARY

autonomic nervous system Part of the nervous system that controls processes such as digestion and breathing.

axon A nerve cell's "tail."

brain stem The brain's "root," at the top of the spinal cord, consisting of the mid-brain, pons and medulla. All signals between the body and brain pass through here.

central nervous system The brain and spinal cord.

cerebellum The billiard-ball-sized lump at the back of the brain, which controls balance and coordination.

cerebral cortex The wrinkly surface of the cerebrum.

cerebrospinal fluid The fluid that protects your brain and spinal cord.

cerebrum Part of the brain where conscious thoughts go on. It registers sensations and tells muscles to move.

corpus callosum The bridge linking the brain's two halves.

cranial nerves Nerves that enter the brain without first going through the spinal cord.

hippocampus A part of the limbic system involved in memories and learning.

hypothalamus The part of the brain that regulates the autonomic nervous system. It controls hunger, sexual desire, thirst, and other feelings.

interneuron A neuron with a short axon.

intuition Knowledge that is instinctive, not reasoned.

limbic system A nerve formation around the brain-stem that links the lower brain and the cerebrum. It deals with emotions and smell.

lobe One of the cerebrum's four parts, known as the frontal, temporal, occipital and parietal lobes.

nerve A bundle of axons.

neurologist A doctor who treats diseases of the brain, nerves and muscles.

neuron A nerve cell.

neurotransmitters Chemicals that transmit nerve signals.

pituitary gland A gland that secretes hormones.

reflex An instant response.

spinal cord A nerve bundle running through the spine.

synapse The tiny gap between two nerve-endings.

thalamus The part of the brain that sends sensory information to the cerebrum.

FURTHER INFORMATION

Web Sites

Digital Anatomist
Includes an interactive brain atlas, with 2D and 3D images.
http://www9.biostr.washington.edu/

Amazing Brain
More advanced information about the brain.
http://tqjunior.advanced.org/4371/index.htm

Brain Backgrounders
Includes an ask-the-expert page on the brain.
http://www.sfn.org/backgrounders/

The Human Brain: a Learning tool
Award-winning educational site.
http://uta.marymt.edu/~psychol/brain.html

Books to Read

Big Head!
Dr. Pete Rowan, Knopf, 1998
Uncover your head, layer by layer.

The Brain and Nervous System
Steve Parker, Raintree/Steck-Vaughn, 1997
Part of a series of books on the human body.

The Human Mind Explained
Ed. Susan Greenfield, Cassell, 1996
A very advanced book, but there are few better reference sources.

The Body and How It Works
Steve Parker, Dorling Kindersley, 1992
Full of fascinating experiments to do.

INDEX